Been There!
SOUTH AFRICA

Annabel Savery

W
FRANKLIN WATTS
LONDON • SYDNEY

Facts about South Africa

Population: 47 million

Capital cities: Pretoria, Cape Town, Bloemfontein

Currency: Rand (R)

Main languages: Afrikaans, English, IsiNdebele, IsiZulu (and many more!)

Rivers: Orange, Vaal, Limpopo

Area: 1,219,090 square kilometres (470,693 square miles)

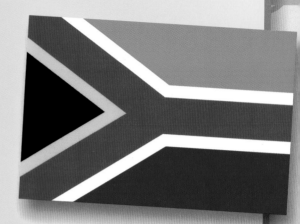

 An Appleseed Editions book

First published in 2011 by Franklin Watts
338 Euston Road, London NW1 3BH

Franklin Watts Australia
Hachette Children's Books
Level 17/207 Kent St, Sydney, NSW 2000

© 2011 Appleseed Editions

Created by Appleseed Editions Ltd,
Well House, Friars Hill, Guestling,
East Sussex TN35 4ET

Planning and production by
Discovery Books Limited
www.discoverybooks.net
Designed by Ian Winton
Edited by Annabel Savery
Map artwork by Stefan Chabluk
Picture research by Tom Humphrey

ISBN 978 1 4451 0353 2

Dewey Classification: 968'.066

A CIP catalogue for this book is available from the British Library.

Picture Credits: p7 (Gideon Mendel), p9 (Tom Fox/Dallas Morning News), p16 (Hoberman Collection), p20 (Matthew Ashton/AMA), p22 bottom (Martin Harvey), p23 (Jonathan Blair), p25 top (Hoberman Collection), p25 bottom (John Hrusa/epa), p26 (Carson Ganci/Design Pics), p27 (Richard T Nowitz); Getty Images: p6 (Eric Nathan), p8 (Neil Overy), pp10-11 (Martin Harvey), p14 (Per-Anders Pettersson/Contributor), p15 main (Clinton Friedman); Istockphoto: title & p24 (Louis Hiemstra), p15 top (FourOaks), p17 (ManoAfrica), p18 (MichaelJung), p22 top (AwieBadenhorst), p29 (jrshein); Photo Library: p13 (P. Narayan), p21 (Peter Brooks), p28 bottom (Tim Hill); Shutterstock: p2 (Michael Roeder), p5 top & p31 (MaxPhoto), p5 bottom (palko72), p12 (MichaelJung), p19 top (Victoria Field), p19 bottom (Leksele), p28 top (David Peta).

Cover photos: Istockphoto: left (ManoAfrica); Shutterstock: main (ShutterVision), right (Abraham Badenhorst).

Franklin Watts is a division of Hachette Children's Books, an Hachette UK company.
www.hachette.co.uk

Contents

Off to South Africa! 4

Arriving in Johannesburg 6

Visiting a gold mine 8

Kruger National Park 10

Exploring Durban 12

At the beach 14

Zulu village life 16

In the mountains 18

A capital city 20

On the train 22

Arriving in Cape Town 24

Up to Table Mountain 26

A fun last day 28

My first words in IsiZulu 30

Words to remember 31

Index 32

Learning more about South Africa 32

Off to South Africa!

We are going to South Africa! This is a country in the continent of Africa.

There are all sorts of places to visit, such as big cities, beaches, mountains, deserts and **plains**.

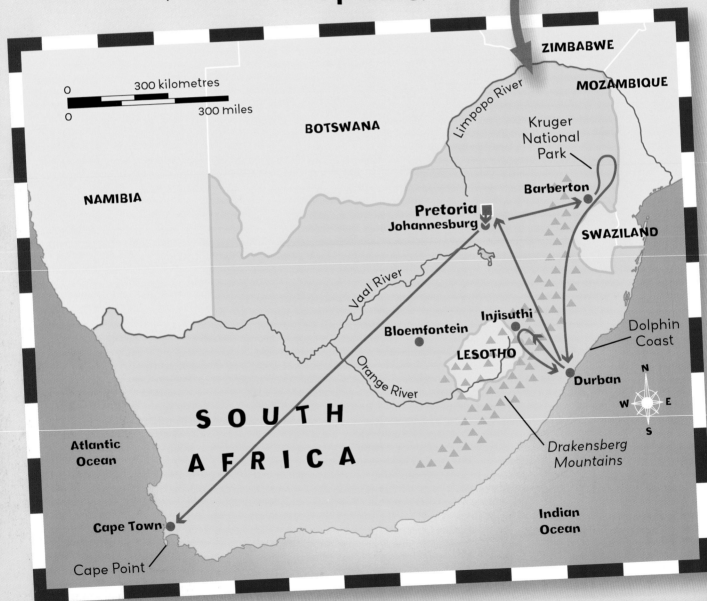

ZIMBABWE

MOZAMBIQUE

BOTSWANA

Limpopo River

Kruger National Park

NAMIBIA

Barberton

Pretoria
Johannesburg

SWAZILAND

0 300 kilometres
0 300 miles

Vaal River

Injisuthi

Bloemfontein

Dolphin Coast

LESOTHO

Orange River

Durban

N
W   E
S

Atlantic Ocean

S O U T H
A F R I C A

Drakensberg Mountains

Cape Town

Indian Ocean

Cape Point

The weather will be mostly warm, but it might also be rainy so I'll need to take a coat. The west coast is usually cooler than the east coast, and the higher areas are cooler too. I can't wait to get there!

Here are some things I know about South Africa...

- **There are lots of wild animals, including giraffes, elephants and lions. I hope we see some.**

- **Lots of gold comes from South Africa, as well as other metals and minerals.**

- **South Africa is called the 'rainbow nation'. This is because of all the different people who live there.**

On our trip I'm going to find out lots more!

Arriving in Johannesburg

Our plane lands in Johannesburg in the morning. We have all day to explore.

From the airport we take a taxi to the hotel. The city is very busy. There are many street stalls selling food and souvenirs.

We drive through an area with lots of very tall buildings. The taxi driver says that this is the main business area of the city. He says that lots of people work here.

Outside the centre there are **suburbs**. Some areas are rich, with big, smart houses. Others are much poorer. These are called townships.

Soweto is one of the townships. We have a guide to show us around. Some parts have nice houses, but in other parts the houses are squashed together and made from sheets of metal and wood.

Visiting a gold mine

The next day we hire a jeep and drive from Johannesburg to a place called Barberton. We are going to visit a gold mine!

At the gold mine we each have a dish and have to swirl muddy water in circles to separate the gold from the mud. I can't find any gold, but I still have lots of fun looking!

Gold is found in many places in South Africa. Gold mines go deep underground into the rock. Some can be nearly five kilometres (three miles) deep! Working in a mine is dangerous and very hard work.

The gold industry has brought wealth to South Africa for a long time. However, many mines are closing because they are running out of gold.

Kruger National Park

The next part of our trip is going to be very exciting. We are going on safari!

We are staying in the Kruger National Park. A national park is an area that is protected by the government. They make sure that animals are not hunted and their **habitats** are not destroyed.

It is fantastic driving through the park. We see lions, leopards and buffalo and lots of other animals, too.

In the afternoon we see a herd of elephants crossing a river with their babies. They are amazing!

Exploring Durban

From Kruger National Park we fly south to the city of Durban. This is the biggest and busiest port in South Africa.

First we go on a boat tour of the harbour. Huge cargo ships and ferries come and go all day long. There are shiny white yachts and fishing boats on the water, too.

A long time ago explorers from many different countries, such as Britain, the Netherlands and India, came to Durban. They brought their styles of building and art here. Their **descendants** live in Durban today.

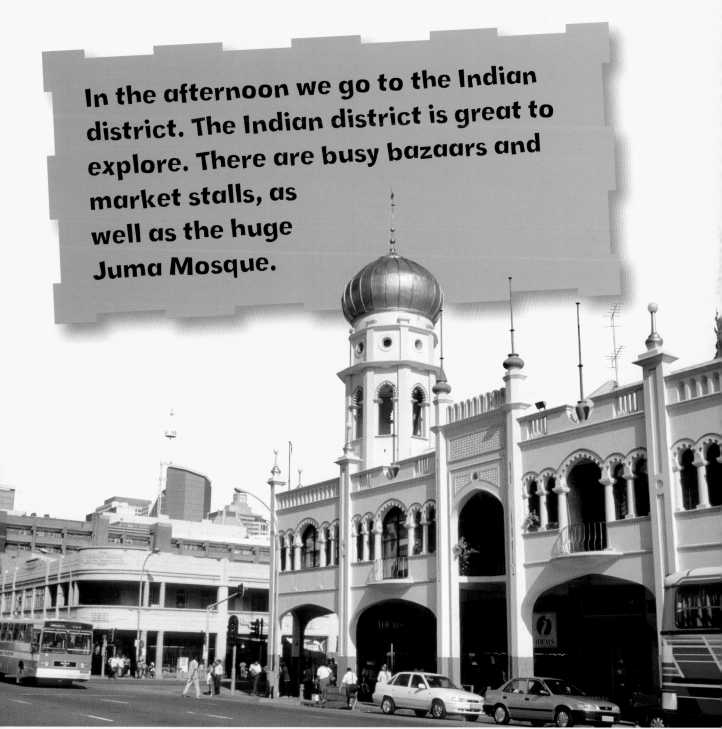

In the afternoon we go to the Indian district. The Indian district is great to explore. There are busy bazaars and market stalls, as well as the huge Juma Mosque.

At the beach

Today we all want to go to the beach. We hire a car and travel north from Durban.

There are beaches to the north and south of Durban. Lots of people come here from Johannesburg and other inland cities.

The part of the coast we're going to is known as the Dolphin Coast. Because the water is quite shallow dolphins live here all year round. I hope we see some.

The sea here is the Indian Ocean. Mum says there are sharks here, too. She says that there are nets in the water to keep them away from swimmers. It's scary swimming when sharks might be nearby!

The sea is lovely and warm. After swimming, we have races up and down the long, sandy beach!

Zulu village life

The next morning, we decide to visit a Zulu village.
Dad explains that the Zulu are people who have
lived in this area for many hundreds of years.

The village is inland from Durban. Zulu
traditional houses are shaped like domes.
Inside they are quite big and feel cool.
The women are wearing beautiful clothes
and lots of coloured beads too.

Some of the Zulu people living in South Africa today still follow their traditional way of life. Others live in the cities and wear western dress, like you and me, instead of traditional clothes.

There are some stalls and one woman is selling clothes made of brightly coloured beads.

The Zulu are the biggest **indigenous** group in South Africa, but there are many other groups too. They all speak different languages.

In the mountains

From the village we travel further inland to the Drakensberg Mountains. The journey takes two hours.

We are staying at a place called Injisuthi. From here we follow a trail that is very steep and leads up into the hills.

The mountains above us are high, with jagged, rocky tops. We can see one of the highest peaks, called Champagne Castle.

We go to see some rock paintings. They were made 8,000 years ago by people called the San. The San lived in the mountains. The paintings show animals and people. It's amazing how old they are!

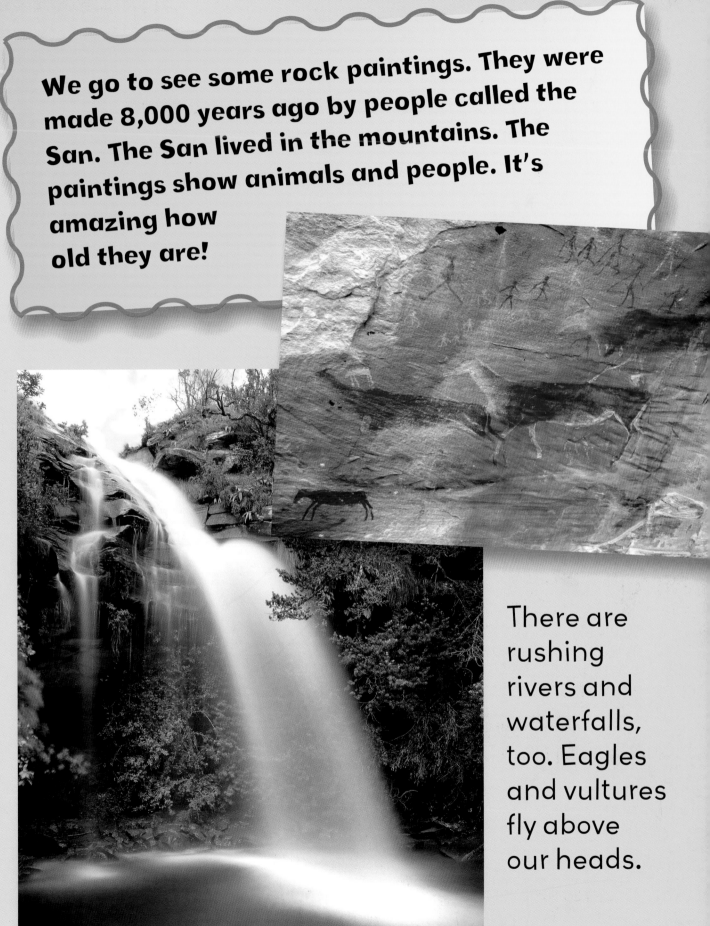

There are rushing rivers and waterfalls, too. Eagles and vultures fly above our heads.

A capital city

After visiting the mountains we travel back to Durban and then fly to the city of Pretoria.

The heart of Pretoria is Church Square. In the centre is a green where lots of people are sitting in the sun. There are important-looking buildings all around us.

South Africa has three capital cities. Pretoria is where the president and his or her cabinet are based; Cape Town is the where the parliament sits; and Bloemfontein is where the Supreme Court is. How confusing!

In the evening we go to a restaurant for dinner. I have *boerewors*. This is a kind of sausage made with meat and spices, and rolled into a coil. It's delicious.

The *boerewors* is cooked on a barbecue called a *braai*. Braais are very popular in South Africa.

On the train

From Pretoria we travel back to Johannesburg to catch a train to Cape Town. We leave at 10.30am and will arrive in Cape Town at lunch time tomorrow.

We pass through farmland where crops, such as sugar cane and maize are growing. Vineyards are planted in straight rows; people are busy working here.

Early the next morning we travel through the Great Karoo. This is an enormous area of dry, flat grasslands. It covers about 400,000 square kilometres (154,440 square miles) of land.

'Karoo' means 'land of great thirst'. Although the area is dry, many types of plants and wildlife live here.

Arriving in Cape Town

When we arrive in Cape Town it is hot and sunny.

Table Mountain towers above the city. There are two other hills too: Lion's Head and Devil's Peak. They act like the sides of a bowl with the city in the centre.

Devil's Peak

Table Mountain

Lion's Head

From the city centre we take a bus to the Victoria and Alfred Waterfront. There are all sorts of boats in the harbour and lots of places to shop and to eat.

We catch a boat from the waterfront to Robben Island. There is a big building on the island. It was a prison and is now a museum. People who were against apartheid were imprisoned here. One of them was Nelson Mandela.

Nelson Mandela later became President of South Africa. In 1993 he was awarded the Nobel Peace Prize.

Up to Table Mountain

It is a lovely, clear day, so we take a cable car to the top of Table Mountain. The cable car is shaped like a fish bowl and it turns as we go up so that we can see all around.

From the top we can see all over Cape Town. From up here the boats moving around the waterfront look tiny.

Back in the city we walk along Adderley Street. This is one of the main shopping streets. There is a market selling lots of handicrafts and clothes, and a flower market.

We all buy souvenirs to take home with us. Mum and I buy some colourful beads. They will remind me of our trip to South Africa.

A fun last day

To the south of the city is the Cape Peninsula. This is a piece of land that stretches into the sea. At the tip are two points, the Cape of Good Hope and Cape Point. This is where we are going today.

The Cape of Good Hope was once a very important place for sailors. Explorers from Europe had to sail past this point to travel further east. There were many shipwrecks here as the sea can be rough and stormy.

On the way back to the city we stop at Boulders Beach. There is a penguin **colony** here. We have lots of fun watching them waddle around!

In the evening we go to a restaurant for our last meal in South Africa. I have *bobotie*. This is a dish with spicy beef on the bottom and egg custard on the top. Yum!

After dinner we pack for our journey home tomorrow. I have had a great time on our trip to South Africa!

My first words in IsiZulu

There are 11 official languages in South Africa. IsiZulu, IsiNdebele and Afrikaans are the most common. Here are some phrases in IsiZulu to get you started.

Sawubona (_say_ **Sawoo boh nah)**   Hello

Hamba kahle
(_say_ **Hambah gah shle)**   Goodbye

Unjani? (_say_ **Oonjah nee?)**   How are you?

Ngubani igama lakho?
(_say_ **Ngoobahnee eegahmah lah khoh?)** Thank you

Igama lami ngu Sam.
(_say_ **Eegahmah lamee ngoo Sam)**   My name is Sam.

Counting 1-10

1 **nye**   2 **bili**   3 **tatu**   4 **ne**

5 **hlanu**   6 **isitupa**   7 **isikombisa**

8 **shiyangalombili**   9 **shiyagalolunye**

10 **ishumi**

Words to remember

apartheid a system where people of different colours or races have to live separately

cabinet a group of officials who give advice to the head of a government

colony a group of animals of the same type living together

descendants people who are the family of people who lived a long time ago

habitat the natural environment of an animal or plant

indigenous people who originally come from a place

Nobel Peace Prize a prize given ever year to a person, or organisation, who has worked towards peace between or within countries

parliament a group of people who make the laws for a country

plains wide, flat areas of land

Supreme Court the highest law court in the country

suburbs the area surrounding a town or city

Index

animals 5, 10–11, 15, 29

Cape Point 4, 28–29
Cape Town 4, 22, 24–25

Dolphin Coast 15
Drakensberg
    Mountains 4, 18–19
Durban 4, 12–13, 14

farming 22
food 21, 29

gold 5, 8–9
Great Karoo 23

Johannesburg 4, 6–7,
    14, 22

Kruger National Park 4,
    10–11, 12

Pretoria 4, 20–21, 22

Robben Island 25
rock paintings 19

safari 10–11

Table Mountain 25,
    26–27
townships 7

Zulu 16–17

Learning more about South Africa

Books

South Africa (Country File) Ian Graham, Franklin Watts, 2004.

South Africa (Learning more about) Rob Bowden and Tony Binns, Hodder Wayland, 2004.

South Africa (Letters From Around the World) Cath Senker, Cherrytree Books, 2005.

South Africa (We Come From) Alison Brownlie Bojang, Wayland, 2002.

Websites

National Geographic Kids, People and places
http://kids.nationalgeographic.com/places/find/south-africa
Geography for kids, Geography online and Geography games
http://www.kidsgeo.com/index.php
SuperKids Geography directory, lots of sites to help with geography learning.
http://www.super-kids.com/geography.html